SWEAR WORDS
&
LOVE NOTES

P.T. BERKEY

For Frank & Susan-

For without you,
None of this
Would have ever existed
At all.

Remy & Peggy-

Thank you for your love, guidance, and care.

DISTANT DESIRES

I live with so many distant desires
Adventures
Sliding right from the top
Of my mind
Ideas and dreams
That have become more like
My religion
Than anything else
My entire being
A mass of
One infinitely interesting universe

I'm just a body
Who at times
Attempts to be mathematical
At understanding
The fleeting pulses
That run through me
Like my blood
Distant dreams
Taken in
As my own
Finding a body
For a home
To act out
Everything
That has not yet
Been.

YOUR BOUNCING NAME

I remember
Just trying to get there,
And the world stood so still
The way that it does-
So I stood next to you
The way that I do-
Hoping you'd see
Just what I'm capable of

And you flinched.

Yet the marquee
Didn't blink.

Instead,
Your bouncing name,
Lit the night sky,
As if you had
Done all of this
Before.
I envied you
For that.

OASIS

We are so busy
Swearing off the unknown
The unseen
The impossible
Trying our best
To be realistic
But
              Everything is amazingly possible

There are things
Wild things
Meeting us halfway
In our hearts
That we must be
Unafraid to look at
And
To chase
These things
Into the darkness
With the fever
Of a thirsty maniac
Hunting an oasis
Of crystal-clear water
In a burning ruby desert.

WILD FLOWERS

I saw a car
Pulled over to the side of the road
While I was driving this morning.
There was a man
Walking up the road
A few hundred feet past the car.
I thought he was going to get gas-
That he had run out,
And I thought I'd stop to give him a ride
To the nearest gas station.

As I got closer
I saw that he had flowers
In his hand-
And was looking down
For more wildflowers
In the clearing
On the side of the road.

I smiled and kept driving.

Thinking
Romance is alive and well.

Give the here and now
As much power
As the thoughts
Of the past
And the future

For it is now
Where memories are made
And the future
Is built.

THE LAST OF THE MOHICANS

I made a box for you
Actually,
A false book that I bought
At some store
"the last of the Mohicans"
It read on the spine.

I put notes, letters
And photographs
That you gave me inside of it.
It's so full
It can barely close anymore.
It's in my closet
In front of other containers
Getting dusty.

But it's just a false book.

People stash cash, drugs, and jewelry in
false books.

I preserve the memory
Of our estranged hope.

CONTEMPORARY MADNESS

We can be
The bright lights
Hands out of the window
In the middle of the night
Pinching space
Between our fingers
In all our glory
As the music from the car stereo
Takes us
And does with us
What it will

No breaks

Just destiny's pistons
Running our souls
Into the rafters
Of midnights excessive peace
Lining our hearts
With contemporary madness
Letting us
Wander upside down
Even if only
For a little while.

LUST FOR LIFE

There are revelations attached to my bones.
There are hues of skies
That swirl in my eyes-
Becoming where we've been
What we have experienced
Tortured ourselves with
And learned through mistakes
Felt supreme joy
In the wake of fortune
And missteps.
We become all of this.
We master the pain.
We ride high
With a hunger for life
Unmatched by any other species.
In it,
A delicate soul
Unraveling and disguising
Unmasking
And shaking the trees.

I long for the amazement belonging to
Every new season
Every shedding of what I was
And the glory
That belongs
To whatever we may become.
I must treat this life in a way
That only I can.
I must remember
That parts of me must be lost
Turning into gentle reincarnations
Of recollection
And fading nostalgic sensations
Of what was
In order to continually fuel this unique lust
For being alive.

Open your eyes.
Let the big, roaring world
Come alive.

ARC OF THE MERIDIAN

Always
I've been watching.
From the outward glances
Thrown about the cabin
In the sky.
The lights off,
Trying to remember where I am,
Where I have been,
But it's easy-
It's easy to steer off into the prai-
rie,
And to chase the sunset
In our cars-
Climb up onto the roof at nightfall
And languish in the heat
Of a beautiful blanket together,
Hoping to find
The stars shooting alive
        Right in front of our eyes.

I'll believe
With you
In the infinite design.
The unobstructed chaos
And our little sight line
Through the hole of the sundial
Resting on your neck-
If you'll let me continue,
I promise it is beautiful.

But we have to
Do it together-
It is the only way after all.

For us,
For the existence of possibility
Seemingly without reason-
We will still be brave enough
To push our unstill hearts
Into the wavering chant
Of an elegant love-
The eyes beholding cold stilts
That have been laying for so long unused-
That the hands that grip them,
Give new life,
To get above the arc of the meridian,
And see that whispering golden horizon
Once more.

IN THE WAKE OF COMETS

Truth be told
      We dance
In the wake of comets.
Brokering deals with ourselves,
So that we too,
Can find our purpose.

And you'll lean cleanly
Against the mantle of your life-
      Gracefully, even.
As if you were supposed to be that way-
Your face four-dimensional
And standing out amongst the photographs
Of your family-
Dreaming in maps,
Tracing lines
Like the veins of an arm
That's been worked hard for years

Us discoverers and seekers,
Shaky participants,
And the ever-brave alike-
      Dialing in
Coming back to ourselves
At unscheduled intervals
Hoping to find a taste-
Of who we thought we were.

Hoping
In the wake of comets,
To live well
And by the code-

      As we reach
For why we're here.

LETTING GO

Insides dim

She answers a call
Of the heart

She heard his sound
His deep tone
Reaching for her

He wasn't there
His sound was gone
She heard a tired sigh
Emerge
From her insides

This is
Letting go.

FILM

Here
The spring exists
Even though the cold
Has taken over

And I give myself room
 To remember
        Everyone in the world
Every solitary place
        At once
        In a blink
Hoping
That I could get there

            For a break
And to come out even

I would give it all that I have
The old world to dusk
Off in a sunset troupe
        Chasing
The end of the world

        The urge
to throw my arms up in the air
out of excitement

To breathe it
Live it
Know it.

TO BE LOVED

I cannot speak for anyone else.
But I believe that there is one thing
That is universally desired
By all people.

And that, my dear,
Is Love.

LET'S SEE THAT HEART OF YOURS

I hope
That it comes up for air-
That it gets exposed
On the surface.
That the vintage lucidity
Of its break-
Swells
And takes part on the surface.

I'll look for it
Shining
Awake
Alive,
Just as it has always been-
But with new light,
At the gala of
Life's ever-changing wonder.
The part where all is governed
Procured and incensed.

Let it breathe
Unashamed & unhurt
Unpacked & unnerved
Let's see that heart of yours.

THE SOUNDS THAT DREAMS MAKE

Her dreams
Sounded like
Soft heartbeats.
Like little feet
Wandering on the floor
Of my mind.
Like champagne
Overflowing glasses
With great friends.
Primrose and peonies,
Clouds and
Soft sands.
Drawn out embraces
And kissing
In silent fields
With the moon
Just behind her head.

Listen.

RADIOCARBON

You run hot
Through your temporal lobe
Stinging from the bad days
Glowing from the good
And seeing that you're still here
To care

And there isn't anything obvious
About you anymore
After going through the war
Never abandoning the ship
Throwing knives against the doors
With the cooks
Drinking beer and singing

There ain't enough for us anymore
To worry about
When you know
You've seen it all before

The sinners
Aren't really
So sinister after all

Maybe just a little lost
Is all.

FERMATA

All the young
All the light hearts
All the starving to live

It's time
It's the witching hour
All that is holy
And sunset-pure
And blushing at compliments
Steers into the lane
Of our stare
All but falling apart
At the knees
With soft dreams
Of open mouths
Pressed against one another's
Reeling in the heat
Of the moments
Basking in the afterglow
Of plush lust
Time does not stop
When we dream of each other

But it sure feels
Like it does.

SLIDESHOW

We let ourselves go
Out into the nothingness
The everything
Brave
As the ones who struck west
Before the west
Was the west
Our eyes tearing through
Every distinct new light
And old flame
In each other's company
Feeling each sight
As valuable
As a lifetime
Of photographs
Left in a box
Being sorted through
By the ones
Left behind.

VIVID

I've acquired
A strong taste
for full bodied memories
And they linger
Like cigarette smoke
And I'm there
Playing
In the second-hand
     Between drags

Letting time
     Pull me to new memories
Before I fall
     To ash
And become a memory
Myself.

PINCHING AT STARS

There we were
        Laying on our backs

Arms outstretched
        My left
        Your right

Pointing
        And pinching
At the stars

Two souls
Light-headed
And light-hearted
        In love

Sending in
        The marching band
From our nectar energies
        To the heavens

And all is right
        In the world

Even if only
        For a moment

I swear
I felt centuries
Sparkling between us
        And the sweet night
sky.

TOMORROW

You might meet
That person
Tomorrow

The one who
Sets your world
On fire

And makes sure
That it burns
In all of the right ways.

GALA DEBUT

There are
Days gone by
In the rearview

Visions
And the promise
Of a future
In the front

A dirty windshield

Getting wiped
In the rain

Windows fogging
With our passions
In the front seat

Some stowaways
And flat leavers
In the back

A gala debut
Right in front of our eyes

All we want
Is a taste

All we want

Is everything.

THE SEAGULL

Under blue skies
I sit
The lonely seagull and I
He vies for a piece of my bread
On our perch
That begins to look like tarmac
For take off
Bay water sloshing on the docks
And the anchored boats sway
And we pray
Eros for your tongue and hand
On a shoulder
If you would-
Bridge the gaps
Between what we see
And that which cannot be yet understood.

SATURDAY MORNING AROUND 830

Sometimes in the mornings
When I got up before you
I would go grab a notebook
Then quietly
Being careful not to disturb you
Get back into bed

My pen to the pages
Scratching away

One day you told me
That when I didn't know that you were awake
You'd watch me sometimes
And that you pictured me
On a beach somewhere
With a drink
Just writing away
And that thought would calm you

Knowing
I was getting my way.

DANAUS PLEXIPUS

A very good friend of mine
Saw his ex the other day-
Opposite his car
Stopped in traffic
While I was talking on the phone with him.
She's a "one that got away" story.
I told him to get her attention
To say hello to her
But he can't.
He's too afraid.
He told me he had butterflies
In his stomach
That she still has that effect on him.
I told him how long it's been
Since a woman
Made monarchs start to migrate
Inside me.
Do not miss this opportunity
I told him
Those feelings are more rare
In this life
Than I like to admit.

You've got to get out there.
It's waiting.
It's all waiting for you.

I DRIVE WEST

I drive west.
Surrounded
By falling sunlight
Embracing
The pink and
Orange hues.
Licking my lips
Goosebumps
On my arms
Back hunched
Towards the wheel
In love
With life
And its tremendous
Magic

I am just going
To keep going

I never want
To stop.

I'VE BEEN BLESSED

I have been blessed
Oh yes, I've been blessed
Hammering through
Knee-deep
In a symphony
Of unstructured obscurity
Looking for my way home
Through dangers high life
Hand in front
Scraping the cobwebs
And running with lions
And the big heart
In a big way
With a big love
Chip off the old blockade shoulder
Melting sweatshops
And jam-packed joint accolades
On the flying mat
With Charlie stardust
And a yoga fanatic
Stands to reason
I've been blessed
Yes sir
Thrift rack giveaway
Lightning rod
Mush maven Iditarod
I'm going to see this
Damn thing
All the way through.

PJ'S PANCAKE HOUSE

I usually refuse
To wait in line for anything.
Impatience
And knowing
Something more interesting
Is probably
Just around the corner.
Plus, we can get pancakes anywhere.
I'll wait though
This time
Because here
We're allowed to write on the tables.
Thousands of people
Left their names in hearts here
And I've got
A freshly sharpened
Swiss army knife
And a poem
With your name on it-
Practically cutting a
Hole in my pocket.

Come here,
I'll take your hand
We'll sneak in through the kitchen
These lines
Are burning up inside,
The one out here is hardly moving.
I hope the cook that I used to know
Still works here.

SUMMER AFTERNOONS

Sadness dies
On those summer afternoons
Hands wet
From beverage sweat
Face getting hot from the alcohol

In decline
And the universe
Is issuing its tell-all
Finally
Much to the delight
Of all the new cast sages

Thoughts change
As do the typesets-
Ambition
Dripping from our chins
Like the juice
Of a properly ripened peach
And what has been given
We accept.
Bondsmen and advocates alike
Clamor
For our eyes-
We need neither.
Soul set free
Upon the hand-cut tile
In the slow drip
Of an electric panel's
Hum.

Somewhere
Something
Someone
Has arranged a meeting
For you and love.

Do not be late.

MESSAGE IN A BOTTLE

It is down there by the water
Where playing children's feet
Glisten from the sun,
Beaming
On splashing little feet
Where the sea glass collects
And the driftwood
Makes its nook in the sand
Where I may have sat hundreds of years ago
With a bottle in my hand
Ready
To throw it into
Her flitting waves
      It was right there
Where the sea glass has collected
And the children play-
And I hope you got the letter in the bottle
Before it came back to shore
And that you still know
All of these years later
That I
      Continue to love you.

IRIDOLOGY

I am obsessed
With the way that you look
When you catch me knee-deep
Staring into your eyes.
Because I know
How wanted you feel–
In these moments,
How hunted
You are.
You sense the longing–
And in these moments,
I sense
You have never been
More ready
To give in.

UNFORGETTABLE

You will remember me
Long after
The last time we speak to one another

My name
Will always live
In the eyes of your mind

In this life
There are only a few
Unforgettables

I will be one of yours
And you
Will be one of mine.

ANGELS EVERYWHERE

Angels everywhere.
And my fire-heart
Lighting the way
The way to everywhere
The infinite openness of the universe
Dialing my number
Asking me where I am
What's taking so long?

I'm here
I'm on my way
Walking the wooden bridges
Across mossy ravines
And bodies of water
Larger than life itself
With love in my eyes

If I move any faster
I'll pass out
Any slower, and I'll faint
If I give myself the time
To look down.

So, this is my speed
On course north
I mean, up
Up to the warm arms of the patchwork
Of the stars
And its perfect fabric

Trying to be present
But saying under my breath
"life is too short man,
Life is far too short."

SKELETON KEY

There was always
Something off about you
Like something was missing
Or hiding
Just beneath the surface.

I should've known
That was the most beautiful thing-
You had probably
Only uncovered it once,
Maybe to the wrong person,
And you'd sworn
To keep it that way
Until the right one
Came along

With the key
That fit your lock.

THESE THINGS WITHIN US

These things within us
That release
Particles
Of imagination
On a trancing
Cosmic spectrum

Somewhere forming
On the rim
Of our galaxies
Beating chests
Delicate
Dried flowers
Finding their way
Along the meridian
Of an unknown universe
Running in lock-step
With our inner eye
Reaching
To find their home

Are the parts of us
That I hope
Never die.

I like my spirals
Downward.
My whiskey shots
Backed up
With a beer
And a fresh cigarette-
My sunglasses
The next day-
My heart, light
My spirit filled,
And my imagination
Left alone
To do its work.

BIRTHMARK ON MY HEART

I don't want to dive
Into your inevitable extinction.
I want to dive
Into your universe of light.
Into your purposeful intent-
The manufacturer of beauty,
The fortune teller inside you
Reading my palm
-telling me I'm going to
Fall in love
With the tracer of my hand.

As if I didn't already know that
As if that didn't already happen
As if you aren't already
A birthmark on my heart.

ROSE COLORED GLASSES

It all falls down around us
Yet somehow
You and I
Stay laying
Amongst a bed of flowers
That we have managed
To carve out
For ourselves
Steady dreaming
Steady loving

Rose colored glasses
And all.

I HOPE YOU FIND IT

I hope
That whatever it is
That you are out there chasing
So long
As it is good and bright
Slows down
Just enough
At just the right moment
For you to catch up with it

I hope you find it
I really do.

AUGUSTE

We cannot pretend
That this life
Is anything less
Than one extraordinary opportunity
To take the day
By the hand
And lead it
Towards every exciting possibility
That we can invoke and dream

One long dance
Of bursting emotions
Trails of feeling
Riding behind us
Like contrails
And the lights
Of a long exposure photograph
The passion
And all-consuming pain alike
The feasts
Our eyes get to gaze upon
When we know where to look
The searching
In all of it
The cycle of oxygen
Hydrogen
Carbon
Nitrogen
Calcium
And phosphorus
Being born
And dying

The unimaginable currents
That nexus us all together
By six degrees

We cannot pretend
That this life
Is anything less
Than incredible.

IT'S IN THE FALLING

It's in the falling.
Where even
the tough as nails
Hardheaded
Swore off love
After the last heartbreak hotel
-Made for life movie
Plays on the last drive thru movie screen
Somewhere in America
The last night of its showing
Because everybody cries at the end-

    Come back to life.

It's in the falling
Of coincidences
And psychic connections
Among two people
Where the soul opens up again
Willing to put itself into jeopardy
Willing to take risks again
Getting high on words
Smells
And the sound of another's voice
Being able to see the perfection
In imperfect things

Because an open mind
And a wise soul know
That this is where
The promise of a future is held.

THE ENDS OF WAVES

There is an elderly man
Holding his grandchild
Near the water at the beach
Swooping the babe
Up and down
Through the suds
At the ends of the waves

I imagine the same man
Eighty years before
Being held
Near the edge of the ocean
Same excited look
On his face then
As he was playing
With his grandfather

Some of the best moments
That the world had to offer
Right there
At the end of those waves.

I DRIVE OUT OF TOWN

Tonight
Is one of those nights
Where the air is perfect
And I drive out of town
With the top down
Chasing something
Trying to look inside
The mystery of the night

    All alone

The energy like
Compressing and expanding neon
Held in the arms of the world
With an Accordian
Pushing and pulling
And I am here
To witness its breath
And the sky
Empties wet lines
That turn into warm tears
Landing on my lap
"look, I cry for you" it says
"look, I cry with you" it says
And nothing is forgotten
In the silky air
The engine burns and shakes
Just like my heart in my hands
        And I want all of it

I whisper to myself
"this is it"
This is everything
And a pure
Confection-eating grin
slides onto my face
Just as I look up
To kiss the sky.

A CALLING

I see milky hills
Dusty skies
Pristine naked emptiness
That I used to walk towards
With pure intentions
Of being amongst nature
And eagerly chasing the spirit
The raw life
The one we were gifted
Man made
Woman made
But not in the sense
That we usually think of right away

Something so powerful
In the atmosphere
Dragging me speechless

A calling to things
I have been
Or need to become.

ETERNAL

Somewhere
In the soul of the universe

There is an eternal love
That never   dies
In fact
It only gets stronger
          As time goes on

Every lover
Every parent
Friend and child
Add drops
Of their beautiful hearts
To the infinite ceiling
Of the galaxies edge
To form stars
That shoot and rain
Across the heavens

Be not still
Our beating hearts.

THEY HAVE BEEN GOING LIKE THIS ALL NIGHT

They have been going like this all night
Plane, after plane, after plane- over the roof of my house.
I lie there in bed – empty, but full of so much.
Dreams soaring over my head. Places I want to go-
Places that I should have gone but haven't yet.
People that I love, and others that I don't-
Running through the space in my mind.
I'm rough with emotion at that moment.
I can't decide what my calling is
Or why I suddenly want to get up and smoke a cigarette-
I "quit" a few months ago.
The night becomes for writing
At times like these.
I have to get out of bed at least
And do my mindless walk to my desk to turn on the computer-
Or cram a piece of paper into my typewriter as fast as I can
While the thoughts still come hot.
I smoke some of my fake cigarette,
One puff every minute or so- it is never lit.
The nicotine must warm me,
It must be my mother's arms.
After I decide my turning thoughts are painful but probably worth
watching-
Observing the hamster wheel spinning until fatigue.
I don't know what I am doing here anymore.
I don't know what I was ever doing.
I pacify my ego momentarily with thoughts of my proudest moments-
A gallery show here or there, a piece of writing that many people
connected with,
And I think I am not such a hack at this life after all.
Hard.
Hard on myself, or far too easy this is what I am trying to determine.
When am I going to run out west again and make a home?
When am I going to keep all of the promises to all of the other warm

blooded
That I have come to know along my lifes-
pan?
The answer is this and always will be:
I will be here,
Figuring this out,
With you,
Until I am not.
Until that day,
I will do my very best-
To try to stay awake.

ALL THERE

This blood is thick
And my skin is so warm
Always, oddly enough.

There are years
That coat my sensitive eyes
Worlds and galaxies
Alive

This body, running through the maze-
Mind attached
And my imagination soars
With grace
Even with ripped feathers
And bruised wings

And if you could see
This goddamn beauty
The way I have
You would be deathly afraid
To ever leave this place too

So, grab me.
And hang on.
Please
Hang on.

I am bound to you
By the stars.

It is simply
The way
That is was designed.

LITTLE CITIES

It seemed kind and warm
The way you would hold
Doors for other people.
The look on their face
As if something
Was out of place.

However,
        Nothing was out of place at all.

It was the warmth
Of another's passing energy and grace
Rising up
Through their body
That pronounced
The wrinkles of their forehead-
Pursed the lips,
Faces
Like little cities.

RING FINGER

The last time
We saw each other
You were off In the distance
Making alibi's
For time lost
Between us
Where the heart
       Had sailed

One hand over
My eyes
Looking for land

There was supposed to be treasure there
The mirage
Of a woman
       I once knew too well
The light
Glistening from her ring finger
       Hit my eye hard

After the sunspots
Subsided
And my boat
Hit land
All that I found
Were your footprints
In wet sand.

SPECKS

We are
The sun,
Moon
& stars.

Down here on earth

Just a reflection
In a puddle

Twirling through
The ocean of galaxies

Playing
With each other's
Hearts.

PIANO AND FRENCH

Up until now
I had always remembered
A piano in my youth
And French lessons
Held in some wonderful woman's home
Just off of route 571

And as I get older
My memories
Are getting trickier to decipher
If they were in fact
Real moments of my life at all

These many things
That when remembered
Hold me momentarily breathless
In awe
And reflection

My right foot
On the sustain pedal
Fingers rolling
On the sharps
And the flats

Bonjour
Je t'aime
Le parfum de cette femme set enivrant
Tu es beau
Merci

In a heaven of visions
Telling the story
Of my dreams
And reality
In united thought
Trying to explain them
The best that I can.

PERFECTLY IMPERFECT

We did it all so perfectly
Imperfect
Blemished memories
And monuments
Like a mesa
Far off in the distance
Of prairie land
Southwest, USA.

Somewhere
Sometime
Somehow
Something
Digging its heels in ya.

Unforced words,
Tongues priming our lips-
And the vinyl cracks
In the background
While we give it our all-
At explaining
Just exactly
What we're doing
Here.

The gossip, lies,
Sex and videotapes
Churning at the end of the reel.

My face flush,
You got me-
God you're so real.
It's the way you look further,
Much deeper
At the creature-
And read well
Before you
Prime your lips
And make me
Crawl to you again

With your everything.

A LITTLE DIFFERENT

Be a little different
In a lot of ways
Let's keep things interesting
And never quit
Hearts like the lights
Over our hometowns
As the airplane climbs
And half circles
Fading gently
Blending
With the night sky
In impossible fashion
And we'll remember
All of the good things
Out loud with each other
Next time I see you
When we're being
A little different
In a lot of ways

Dripping our hearts
Like burning candles
No two alike
No feeling the same
Just us and the light
Feeling the truth
Of one another
Even if only
For one last night.

REVOLUTION

There will be a revolution
A revolution of love
It will not be televised
It will not be commercialized
Or be presented
By corporations
Or celebrities.

The revolution of love
Will be quiet
And organized within
There will be enough love
Pointed outward
Towards the great universe
That the world will see
Love
Is all that really matters.

Maybe
I am just
Tortured, distant,
&
Beautiful

FIREWORKS BEHIND MY EYES

We are the dreamers
The visionaries
The ones ready at a moment's notice
With our bags to boogie.
To move,
To get going,
To dance with life
And everything
That it has to offer.

All of the incredible people,
The places we've been,
The ones we haven't yet-
But can practically
Taste
See
And feel.

The colors
The energy
The everything
It's waiting-
It is
The fireworks behind my eyes.

SITTING QUIET

I sit quiet
       In attempt
         At meditation
 I relax
       I close my eyes
     Staring at the darkness
        Behind my eyelids
Trying not to think
       Just to see
The fragments of life
       Passing before me
          Specks of light
       The lighthouse
And the shadows
       Of the quiet mind
  And resting body
Sinking
Gazing
Still.

FRIDAY NIGHT

Paper cut-outs
And ashtrays in mid-90's diner booths
Electric cigarette smoke like a buffer
Between bad breakups
And love stories starting anew.
Somewhere
Destiny catapults your wavy airs
Around in the night
And the light-colored coasters
At dead dive bars
Get filled up
With way more than telephone numbers.
Who knew
That you could learn so much
From a tipsy stranger
With a Bic pen
That's got teeth marks on the end
With the cap
Now somewhere in the ice that
The bartender is using
To make Vodka soda's
All night long.
Life is a study, my friends
And we each have two sides-
Juxtaposed blindly
By some holy genius
Somewhere giggling at
Its magnificent experiment.

ALL MY PIECES

With all of my pieces
Laid out beside me
My shallow void
And my excesses
My true
My cover
My blending
Of the show

      I arrive at now.

I have come for the world
      To row the stream of consciousness
To allow my tide
To wash over you

One last time.

BORN AGAIN

I have seen the way you look at me.
As if you're intending on keeping me forever.
It excites me
And scares the shit out of me
At the exact same time.

You see, I've convinced myself that I wasn't
built for forever's.
I'm so used to being left, and leaving
Without so much as a hint
Or a fair warning of any sort.
I'm not sure if this is learned behavior
Or I just really don't know
How to hold onto things.
But that look of certainty you give me
Just before you lean up to kiss me
At the most random moments

Makes me feel so at ease.
I'm older now, I tell myself.
I've learned so much from failure.
I've been to some therapy
opened up
And been put back together- somewhat.
So, when you look at me
Like you believe
And I look back
And see honest eyes in earnest
Truth and sturdiness
I tell myself
I am willing to get up
And try again.

BEAUTIFUL STRUGGLE

Here we are
        Together.

Living
    Breathing

In this part
Of the beautiful struggle
                With one another

As fate would have it
        No other way.

AGING

Over time
The fine lines
Of the sun's rays
Have found your face

The rings
Of the moons glow
Have settled
Underneath your eyes

The white caps
Of the tallest mountains
Have begun descent
Upon your hair

And when you think
You are getting closer
To leaving this place

The salt from the oceans
Runs down your cheeks
To your feet,
But do not worry

We are just
Riding the wave.

RUBBERNECK

Driving
And there's a rake in the road
Everyone drives right up to it
Slows down a little
Then runs over it
The speed limit is only 25

An older man
Pulls his car over
And gets out
I don't know
If he needs a rake
Real badly
I know fall just passed
Or maybe he just wants
To get it out of the road
So people don't have to
Brake and swerve

No one stops
They just slow down
Run over it
Or swerve
Into the other lane
To avoid it
A hundred cars
Must have hit this stupid plastic rake
But they can't just let him
Pull the rake out of the damn road
No, that would slow them down even more

After all
It is the holidays
And we all have

Very important things to do
I like where the older man's head is at though
If it wasn't for people like him
No one would ever stop
Until something bad happens
And they can rubberneck
As they drive by.

RANDOM ACTS OF MEDITATION

Sell everything
Run towards the unknown
Learn a new language
Talk to strangers
Study the way a child smile's
And looks at their surroundings
Give
Just because you can
Have another drink
Stare into people's eyes
Stop and look up
In the middle of the day
Play it by ear
Don't be so fuckin serious
Hit the stairs running
Lay down in open fields
Even if it's snowing
Read out loud to your lover
Stare at them
As if they
Are the only person in the world
Write notes to them
And hide them
Where you know they might find them
Listen to a record
Try to climb a tree
Really listen to what people
Are trying to say
Practice random acts
Of meditation-
Breathe.

HOPEWELL BUCK

I am
The starlight wonder boy
Lust for life
Tattooed on my arm
Jimi Hendrix guitar pick
Swinging around my neck
Pushing across
The heartbeat
Of a small American town
In a rusted Dodge farm truck
Three speed on the column
Salvaged from a barn

The old man
Who used to own it
Couldn't wait
To see me running
Those baby blues
Up and down main street
Mind firing
On all cylinders
Hummingbird brushstrokes
Of my tongue
Just under my breath
So never too out of tune

And everywhere that I go
There are spoils

You just have to see them
You just have to believe friend.

WRITTEN IN STONE

In all of the magic
That is us

There is carved
In stone
A story

Hidden somewhere
      A human's eye
Has never been

And a chisel
      Driven by
An invisible force
That works tirelessly
To transcribe
Our love story

      One moment
At a time.

WHILE WE'RE HERE

Albeit strange,
It is ours.
We give each other
Our words
And some things
                    Even keep promises
To one another
Along the way.

It isn't fair,
You know that
It just isn't fair

That we'll do
All of this-
Perfecting,
Losing,
Fighting
To hold things

That like us
Must eventually
Leave.

PAUSE

Where are you now
As you sit there spinning
With the world

This perpetual state
Taking us
Blindfolded
With our eyes inside
Our only guide

Where will you be tonight
When the sun moves out
And the curtains come down
Always deciding
What to do next

Where is the pause

Where can we retreat
To truly let our
Energies rest
Before we slip
Out into the ocean
Of sleep
Again

Going, going, going,
Gone.

Goodnight,
Tomorrow is another day
To dizzy
And quiet ourselves
Again.

I have found that two things always seem to come back to me:
All of the good things that I have done-
And all of the bad things.

In no particular order.

RICH LIKE THE HEAVENS

Somewhere in the cross stitching
Of the orchestra
That is your life-
Between the finding and falling,
Purveying objects &
Always noticing the way that moods bloom-
Eye on the stamen
Prize in your pocket
Hearts on the concrete
Next to overturned scoops
Of ice cream-
We're rich like the heavens darling.

The astrological constellations
Like maps
Pulsing in the night-
And there is a moment
Where your unceasing energy
Has no choice
But to be still-
        And to watch the ceremony unfold.

Heavy on the breath
And the sensation
Of your chest-
Thrusting gently at the sky
Giving in to possibility

These moments are few in our lifetime-
Proceed accordingly.
But most certainly
Proceed.

STILLNESS IN FALL

Just as the leaves
Begin to fall
All around us
Just as the wind
Pushes against my face
      I stand still
I stand
      Allowing myself to feel
Where I am now
      This is me
No judgements
No worrying
No rushing to the next appointment
      Or creating more.
This is the most distilled and pure
Form of existence
The silence
The quiet
 The now
Just as everything is falling
      All around us.

ESCAPE ARTISTS

I don't think
This was meant for us

We
Who cannot handle
      The mundane
And
Living someone else's dreams

Let us
Get out of this place

Let us
Become known as
The greatest escape artists
That have ever lived.

ART NOT WAR

Let's make love and art
not war
let's blow each other's minds
with paint
all over our bodies
outstretched
on canvas
flat
on the kitchen floor.

SOUL CHANTS

I remember those nights
Standing in Luke's living room
With the blackboard.
A bunch of maniacs
In their late teens
Scribbling everything that our souls chanted
And rattling off wild poems and ideas
Like lightning
On those cool, spring nights.

The fires in the backyard
Were probably just as glorious
As when Jesus walked
In the middle east.
That wine,
And those girls
All went straight to our heads-
And barely put hair on our chests
Before we would all retreat
To couches and sleeping bags
After kissing
And smoking ourselves to sleep.

Those memories remind me
Of what I was becoming-

Alive.

AMONG THE TREES IN THE RAIN

I'll be whistling through the storm
Staring out of the car window
At the trees in the rain
Dying for a nature walk
Brushing up against the leaves-
The woods provide such a beautiful canopy
During the downpours.

I'll be madly in love with all of it
No time for my waterproof notepad
Field-rated
Fury-tested
For the fast longhand
Of a gentleman
From Tortuga
With a splash of honey in tow

And you danced in the late thirties
Somewhere with me-
It all comes back in the rain
Divine sight
To the man
They say still has his boyish charm
And an air of mystery about him
Undefined
I must go in now
I must be in the forest
In these heavenly rains.

ALL OF IT MAKES YOU BEAUTIFUL

She said "where's that one from?"
"ahh, that's from when I was five or six
Playing in the tree in the backyard
With my friend.
He was at the top of the tree
And dropped his chopstick
From the Chinese food
(it was supposed to be a sword)
And as I looked up, it fell
Right into the edge of my eye.
My mom had to give me a few sips
Of a rolling rock or Heineken
To calm me down before she pulled it out."
"What about that one?" she asked.
"That's from when I flipped
Over the handle bars of my BMX bike
With a stolen stop sign under my arm."

She just looks at me endearingly
Seeing the wild child in me
And smiles.

There are so many scars,
Burns and bruises.
But I don't care about those anymore, really.
"right here" I said,
As I put my hand over my chest-
"this is where the worst of 'em are.
No one ever really asks about those
Because you can't see them."

"I can," she said.
"and all of it makes you beautiful."

JACKIE

The short way of it is this:
You've been carried thus far
To take what you can
Then go.
There's no lingering
No hanging out at the top
Reciting your laurels
Slamming on drums.
Just go peacefully
If not willingly
Sing your song to yourself.
If you're lucky
There will be a couple or three
Still there
Willing to listen
And maybe
Maybe
Even hummm along.
I remember how Jacqueline broke.
We hummed her song
To my grandfather's ghost
The last thing she told me
Was to enjoy my life.
"Live, really live your life"
And
She wouldn't get on me
If it rhymed.

UNTIL THE WORLD CATCHES FIRE

They won't make movies about us
They won't smoke herb
While listening to our music
Stoned
In their favorite armchair
They aren't going to
Crow and ponder
Every stroke of our brushes
At the metropolitan museum of art
We won't be immortalized
In a house of wax
Or
Have our names in some Hollywood slab

But hell,
If we weren't brilliant together.

They can find our stories
In our ink stained pages
Where we'll live
Until the world
Catches fire.

I DO NOT WONDER

I do not wonder
  Why we are scared so often
  Anymore-

     To show our hearts
        Our dreams
        Our faults

What they will never
  Teach us in school
Is just how difficult
     It can be to love-
When it appears that as time goes on
  It becomes easier
For people to walk away
  From us-

        Hardly batting
          An eye.

I choose
Not to err
On the side of caution.

I've lived
Most of my life
Like this.

Never knowing
Where the night
Might take me,
Crossing my fingers
That it doesn't
Swallow me whole.

NEVER LOSE YOUR WILD

In an increasingly stagnant
And starchy world-
It is easy
To forget ourselves-
Who built this thing,
Who we are,
We who have left the wild behind us
In hopes
Of some gleaming prize
For following
The status quo.

We may have lost our creativity,
And dare I say-
Our edge.
We've lost beautiful parts
Of ourselves,
And it is not okay.

Find it.
Find it fast.
Before it blends in
With the horrible tile
On that perfect, cheap
Floor.

Save yourself.

Never lose
Your wild.

I cannot help
But think
Of the magnificent change
That could take place
In the world–
If only
We could learn
To love,
Beyond our means.

BILLET-DOUX

I had a big love.
A big love
For everything
And everyone.
       All of it-
The damned and the angels
And the tired drunk saints
That were somewhere in between.

The glory and the evil,
The struggle and the triumph,
That exists between
Everything being chased
From one spectrum
To the next.

You need to have a big love
To get on in this life-
And if you're lucky,
You might just find a big love

Right within your soul.

BLUE BOTTLES

I've been dumping courage
Out of this thing (me)
Since my art teacher (Dave)
Told me that I was a badass
In the third grade
At a Quaker school (friends)
In New Jersey (home)
"Just give them your truth, no matter how it comes out."
He told me
On his way to string blue bottles
From the phone poles
Of my youth

I don't know
If I was listening
Then

But I am listening now

Just enough to let it go
And run itself wild (spirit)
Through the streets
And the fields

Of my inner worlds.

CONSIDERATE

I will think of you
Even at times
Where it may not seem to matter at all.
I expect nothing-
                              So do not think I am carrying weights
                    With me.

            When I come
            I may offer you help
                    Solace
                    Friendship, love
Whatever I have
            At the time-
            However
None of it
            Is really good enough
            For you-
You
Are that wonderful.

SAVE OURSELVES

In the golden age of man
I was well curated
Sterling silver
A lone rock
Jutting from the oceans face
Wanting everything
To not be golden
Out of reach
Out of touch
Trying to see myself
And my fellow people
For far more
Than a link
In the fence
Built around paper mache castles-
Knowing full and damn well
That if we're going to be saved
It's not money
Politics or god
That's going to do it
Or even stand up for us-
But ourselves,
We the people,
Who can only save us
From our heavy
Man-made molds.

Next time you feel so alone,
Don't.

For you are alone
With the rest of us lonely souls.

TENDERNESS

Have you ever lost it all?
Your family, friends, money, your mind,
Or all of your things?

Have you ever stolen
Or begged in the street
To feed yourself?

Walk down the street,
Anywhere in the world-
You will inevitably pass someone
Who has lost a loved one.

You will pass someone
Who has a mental illness,
Someone who has lost their home.

I wonder
If we can look at one another
A little differently sometimes-
Look at everyone we come across
Without judgement or assumptions.

Because the truth is:
We only know what people tell us.
We only know what people
Are unafraid to say.

Let this be an experiment
In tenderness.

Keep the magic alive.

X X X V

You stood in line
At the DMV
Waiting to do some type of paperwork-
"Next," the agent calls out loudly, over my thoughts of what you
must be like
            You inch closer to the window
            Like the rest of us
                        But I knew
            You weren't like the rest of us.

            I plot my move to get your attention
You make it through the first gauntlet
Of DMV hell
And then are told to wait until your number is called.

I craft a note on state-supplied scrap paper
While I get funny looks from the clerk-
"You're so beautiful" the note said.
My nerve and anxious stomach spasms could only let me
Drop the note at your feet as I left the building-
"I think you dropped this." I said. I picked up the note,
Handed it to her, then walked away.

It was raining, so I ran to my car and drove away-
What if? Drumming in my head.
                  I turn the car around and go back.

In my car, I write another note with the Roman numeral II at the top-
Then I go back inside to find that luckily
            You were still there- sitting in the same place
            With a big grin on your face.

I give you the second note, I introduce myself
And we exchanged phone numbers this time.

I fell in Love that day.

We made it up to XXXIV.

MAKEUP

I am part evening drives
Some type of optimist
Generally
A caring and sweet person
Chaser of beauty
In many forms
Embracing the tough to watch along the
way too
Finding it hard to be a believer
Sometimes at my age
Not ok with giving up
Singing quietly by myself
Twice a year or so
When I feel beyond peaceful
Or extra spun and worked up inside
Kaleidoscope admirer
Daydreamer
Of the truest kind
The guy
That talks to the old man
Sitting by himself
At the bar
Field walker
Train sleeping car enthusiast
Into classic cars
Even though sometimes
I like to think that
I'm above that
Chameleon
Of social situations
Famous
For my Irish goodbyes
Family oriented
Yet still single

With no children
The one who will look into your eyes
So long as I can tell you aren't evil
Or have malicious intent
Trusting my instincts
Going where I feel I should
Leaving notes for loved ones
Along the way
Understanding that life is hard
For all of us
And some
Much more than others
Taking my time
Taking it all in
Hanging on to my oldest friends
Being true
Patriarch
Misunderstood saint
Battle tested
Sitting quietly
Observer
Of the
Here and now.

GENTLE SONG

When I saw you standing there
That fateful day
The song you sang
Just quietly
Under your voice
Warmed my soul
I left a note at your feet
As I couldn't look at your face
For too long
Then later that evening
You sent a picture of the note
On your bedsheets
And we made some plans
I stashed notes and flowers
In secret boxes
To warm your soul
And somewhere on the horizon
Your eyes lit a dark castle
And a romance
Was born.

THEY'LL NAME SKIES AFTER YOU

They'll name skies after you
        I swear

It's one of those things
They should tell you
When you're a child

Because they want you to know
That everything
        Is possible
Because it is.

It is only the coming of age
And the ridiculous realities
That we face in the interim
That douse those ideals
In the dregs
Of lost hopes

We need to maintain the faith-
Every time we learn something
That partly unteaches our innocence
        We must do our best to forget it
To move forward
And revive our youthful imaginations
The best way we can

They'll name skies after you
I swear.

FROZEN

Each turn
In the drive
Sends new flashes
Of beautiful mad waves
Through me
Images
Never to be seen again
Perfect in time
Frozen photography
Flickers
Of solitary moments
That will soon flush
With the paper-

The only way
To prove
The moment
Ever existed at all.

I AM HERE

I stay quiet near the back
Understanding loosely holds me in the rhythm
Of the goings-on tide
Specks of the past dot my tired brain
And it pumps wholly at the same time
With energy blending
Between my hearing and sight
And I press my index fingers onto my ear canals
Then release
Press
Release
Hands over my eyes
Then away
Peek a boo
It never stops
I wake up in the middle of the night
As if I was sleeping at all
And in the morning
All of the pillows are off the bed
And I am sideways
I am beside myself
                    I am here.

What the world sees of you
Is surely not all that you are-
Just as what you see of the world
Is surely not all that it is.
Show yourself
Keep your eyes open

And your compass out.

KICKING & PUSHING

Do you hear the subtle sounds
Inside of you?
The stories and songs
Of your youth
The kids on swings
Kicking and pushing
Trying to get enough momentum
To jump right out of their seats

Knocking on your doors
The doors of your mind
The music of your soul
Pushing to escape
To get out in the world

And learn to express itself.
Let it out
These sounds
Of your soul
      Without being afraid
If they translate or not.

LITTLE WORLDS

There is a fountain
With a smaller, round, stone pool
With just enough water
To get your knees wet
Just enough water
To flick with your thumb
Small denominations
Of coins-
and if you are with a child
You must use
Any coin that you can,
Insert imagination
And be free
Even from the money
At least for a moment.

The tin cans between trees
Are calling.
When a bush was a world
And a coin in a fountain
Was a dream.

BORED COUPLES

I see bored couples at the bars
At the restaurants
They talk a little bit
But they look like they have to reach
Just to keep it alive
They judge every single person in sight
And make up stories
About what their lives must be like
And smirk at their outward appearances
Not because they really want to
Just because that's really all that is left
Don't focus on me
I won't focus on you
They are listening but
Listening is used very loosely these days
I choose to listen
To the people I am with
Because if I am with you
I genuinely care enough to listen
To truly hear you
Otherwise I'd be alone.
So, what makes you stop hearing the one you're with?
Or did you ever hear them at all?
I don't want to be anyone's judge
But it's far too difficult for me not to see
And to try to understand the gray areas
That lie everywhere in life-
Especially in human beings.

It's just that
We are all so much more
Than glances across
A bar.

BANDITO

You know what I wanted to do
I wanted to sit somewhere quiet with you
And just have a beer
And talk
About whatever is going on in your life
In great detail
I want to know all that's going on
And how it's affecting you
I want to know how your family is doing
What your latest ventures are
What you have planned for the future
What is your latest dream
And if there is anything special
That I can send the kids for the holidays
And you'll ask me about work
And how my art is going
If I've been seeing any new girls
-and I'll tell you that I just haven't had the time
We'll remember
And drink
And for a few hours
There would be nowhere else
We'd rather be.

I miss you man.

HANG ON

This world
Can easily drive us all mad
If we let it-
It's a tightrope we walk
A constant balancing-act
And we're in the thick of it.
Just trying to find
People
Places
And things
To hold on to-
So that we don't lose
Our precious minds.

MUSCLE MEMORY

Staring down this highway
Toward new paths
Trying to plot the future
Torn
Between comfort
And the excitement
& fear of the new
The unexplored
The wonder
Of becoming undone
Put back together
Between these two places
Moving constantly
In pose
And pressing love
Unto others
Slightly paralyzing
The way that you seem to do that with such grace
You'll too be carried through
This great journey
To places you haven't even had
The pleasure of trying to pronounce yet
All the while
Combing the shores of your aura
For clues
The air against the windshield
Driving on that highway
Allowing your soul to trust itself
To take you wherever
You may need to be

In the process
Don't you know
        You'll move me.

FIERY ENERGY

That empty space
Above your soft palm
Sends quivering pulses
To my open hand
Longing
For your touch
To bridge the gap
Of our Fiery Energy
And feel one
Again.

I can say with great certainty
And absolute honesty
That I did not know
What love was
Until I knew
What love was not.

NATURAL DISASTER

I've been through storms
Strong enough
To kill people
Brought to my knees
In the forevermore
In the buffed out
Writing on the wall
All while trying to understand
Only to realize
That the world doesn't stop
For anyone
For anything
And nature
Reigns its great strength
Down onto us
Which we are not able
To full comprehend.
Funny,
We are so much like nature.
The way we are
The way we react
As if without consequence.
We are so much like nature
It hurts.

RIGHT WHERE THEY COME IN TO LIVE

I imagine words
        Being pushed like breath
From the mouth

        Turning into a gust of wind
        Blowing through the homes
On hills
  In some coastal town
Far and away
        From where I am at this very moment.

        And I want to be there.

I want to be in the alleys
Side-streets
        And the small places.

In the windows
& on the rooftops
Among the people
And especially the lights in the evening-

        Where words are everything
        Right where they come in
To live.

LAUREL FIELDS

We still believed in the wide open
The allure
Of lying down on countryside fields
Under the star drenched skies
Captivated
By the slow walk
To where
Our woven blanket
Would be placed in the stillness.

Knowing
How vast the galaxy was
Yet in some way
Feeling as though
We were the center of it all.

ALOE DIPPED EYES

The future looks at me
With aloe-dipped eyes-
The trees sway
In innocence unrivaled
And the dream catching
And letting go
Does not end.
Head in the clouds
Feet on the ground
Imagination spinning me
In soft semi-circles
That defy dimensions and time.
The ever-elusive peace
And sense of purpose
That always seems so far away-
Right under our very own skin
Yet we cannot accept that.
Ambient sounds
Of the pool party
In the background
Smokey looks
Drunk angels-
You are that
That is I.

DRIED ROSES

If you knew

Just how long
This boy
Has Been waiting

Impatiently
Biting my nails
And smoking cigarettes
Pacing
In my sleep

Trying to unwrap presents
Without tearing the paper
Just to get a peek

Staying up all night
Wondering
When it's going to happen
When
Will
The
Stars
Align

If you knew
How many times
I've fallen
And gotten gagged
With my own roses
After they'd dried up

You'd wonder
How I still

Have enough
Drops of hope

To wait for you

To fill
Your empty ocean.

A wise
And very true person
Once told me:

"you're in the best possible position
That you can be in-
You've got
Nothing to lose."

AMETHYST & AMBER

My mom waits for me
The way a mom waits for her
Son
                    Patient
Like what we're becoming
                              Her & I

I can't think of 6 days
That have gone by
That I don't think of moving
    Out to California
            Get to know my sister
                    All over again
Even though either of us
Has hardly changed.

Honestly, I think that's how
        I like it

Sweet, swift, and
                    A couple road trips
            Between us
                    Love pushing through the atmosphere
                Thru a channeling machine road surfboard
            Jeep emblem
Forcing Wyoming tunnels shut
With intention
Will of mind
Under mountain
Over matter
Mind high yield
Never suitcase
Unforgiving end of beginnings
Keep her up talk
To the fruit inspection toll
At the Cali border
And we sing-

KINDNESS

The part of you
That I would come to love most
Was not your face
Not the way you make me feel
Not your mind
With all of its gorgeous
Thoughts
It was your kindness
To me
To all living things.

I have definitely
Gotten lost
In your eyes.

I have definitely
Found myself
In them too

MODALITY

The color of your memory
Is sky rose
And the sounds of your feet
Like a ballerina
Sliding down slate rooftops
In the see-through armor
Custom made
To deflect the calm urgency
Kept in cayote night calls

Frozen fountain pen promises
And sealed kisses
Pressed on linen paper
With a spritz of that parfum concoction
Hand crafted from your majestic taste bud back arches

Hearts on the nightstand
Guns tattooed on ring fingers
Interlocked and weaving
Like infinity
In front of recurring nightmare waterslides
Me and mischievous miss
Holding up the line to gender specific bathrooms
You leave first
I'll walk out two minutes later–
Gotta check my hair.

LITTLE BRANCH

There is a little speakeasy
In New York city
That I used to go to pretty regularly.
On a Tuesday night
I could catch one of my oldest friends
playing guitar
With his Jazz trio
And I'd get a couple drink tickets.
And while they played
Sweet sounds of the upright bass
Strings and sweeps
Of the drummers brush and snare
I'd tap my foot softly
Next to a woman
While I tried to
Capture the moment
With a drink in hand
Spilling on my now bittersweet fingers
Burning longhand
On the back of a coaster
Soaking up life
And all the faces
In the candlelight
Murmuring their own tunes
To their friends or lovers
In the sweet sounds of that
Basement music room.

RECKLESS

If you'll believe
In all of it
Until the end of centuries
Until there is no more
Hanging on to the lightning rods
Casually photographing
These perfect moments
Eyes like lens and shutter
Holding one another
To the light
In nights soothing reach
Counting our blessings together
Against pillows
And staring at the ceiling
Open-eyed and remembering
Courteous and blunt
Minding the fire
Using the unimportant things
That we've so innocently
Wasted our time on
To feed and burn like kindling
So that we can get deeper
And more relevant
Hanging on to the constants
Making sure
That we never lose
the hot fever
Or that if we do
We are able to make strong comebacks

I'll believe too
Recklessly as ever.

WHERE AM I?

I do not know
What is expected of me
anymore
I do not know
What
I expect from myself
From you
From life even-
One continuous question,
And we,
Forcing our way through,
Find ourselves
Here.

Why

Why
Am I here?
With thoughts
The rate
Of six million
Bolts of lightning
Trying to stare
Them in the face

Terrified
Of the fight
Often times
Of swinging first
Or even
Learning how to box

Yet still
I am here

Trying to understand

What is expected of me,
What I expect from the world.

I AM THE GUN

I am the gun
I am the peace sign
Being made with a hand
I am driving
Listening to soul music
Bobbing my head
I am rock n' roll
I am tight lipped
Telling secrets
I'll labor until I can't feel my feet
I am lazy as hell
I am spiritual
I have never met a god
I am perfect embrace
I have shoulders like ice
I remember how sweet summers taste
I can't remember what I ate and drank last week
I am so afraid of dying
Yet
I know that one day
I'll be too tired to be afraid

I am manicured gardens in the countryside
I am fight club
I am the expectation
I am the disappointment
I am
A little bit
Of everything.

I've got promises of way past midnight with you
Written all over my wild eyes.

HERE'S TO LOVE

The truth
Of any man
Woman and child
Is that they need to be loved-
To pursue their dreams
To have compassion for all
To live a rich life-
It is love that can hold us up
Love,
That can transform an existence
So,

Here's to love.

PAST LIVES

I remember that time
You sent me a song
That you wanted me to listen to
And I did
It was a beautiful song
I went to a party later that night
At someone's house
There were a lot of people there
But not you

There were
Drinks flowing
The music was going
And I thought of you
& the song you sent to me

I stuck it on the stereo
Sat in front of it
And listened to it
In my own world
At a party
Everything in slow motion
Just thinking
How beautiful life can be
When I'm
Thinking of you.

THE FORGE

We push through
The ways
     We know how to-
   Truthfully, gently,
  Hard, fast, soft,
    Sometimes willingly
  And unwillingly.

Saying to ourselves
  That we're going to make it-
And we do.

     We will, we can,
    We must.

WE'RE ALL CHASING SOMETHING

We're all chasing something

    And I'm chasing myself
Upper east side
The countryside
It's all the same

Writing and rewriting
Dodging bullets
And eagerly
Faceplanting into kisses

And if you understand it all
Any better than I do
Well, bonus

No more orders in my words,
No
Just sunset chasers
Wild dreamers
And the doldrums

I let it write for me
For long enough
Then the horse got loose
The horse got loose
Oh, little runner,
Little told all by the fireside
What'd ya know?
That the fire burns
'Til all the logs are embers

Let me be blessed
Let me burn
And
Let me learn my embers.

When you find something you love-
Love until the doors fall off.
Then put 'em back on
And love some more.

THE DANGER IN YOU

You put Spanish fly in my drink
And melt Harlem
With wet kisses
You picked up at the loosie spot
Right around the corner
From where we used to get
Those little vials of hydro
After nervous train rides
From the fireworks lady
In Chinatown

The danger in me
Seeks the danger in you

So tomorrow
We can go play
Where our edgy eyes meet
At precise moments
Of knowing

During the day
We'll praise one another
Work diligently
Help the world
Get things done
Make some money
And fuck off a lot too

But during the night
I'll grab your hand
And we'll make
A break for it
So you can melt the world
When our eyes meet

At precise moments
Of knowing.

LONELINESS

I have the urge to go buy something
or
get into a heavy night of drinking or drugs
or find someone to sleep with at least

medicine for loneliness
temporary things
that I don't actually need
I guess I've started to grow out of that
I start to let it go

I've bought my fair share of useless shit
I've had way too many nights of poisoning
my body
And I don't want to sleep with just anyone
Maybe I'm just far away from myself
And trying to find my way home
Disconnected
And worn out
From looking for so long
I tell myself
"you just gotta let it pass man,
Just let it go."

Loneliness isn't forever
But I need my medicine
So
I take it back
I'm going to go buy something and
Have a drink

But I'll still sleep alone.

AT ALL COSTS

I find it much harder to pretend
That I'm not
As good
As bad
As ugly
And beautiful
As I am
Than just giving the world
The brute force
Of my real
My everything
At all times
At all costs-
Stay true.

I work
With
My hands.

I build,
I write,
I talk,
I create,
I curse,
I paint,
I swear,
I love.

I work.

HARD

We were fit to wear the mat down
Even in our weakest moments
Letting our soul colors
Run through-
                And we had been
          At our high moments too

The worlds stage ran Coltrane-blue

Doves
And the lovely sore eyes
At the tavern
Sworn-in hand
Grinding on the barnacles
And all of a hard life lived

Tell-tale signs
         Wearing us down
At & underneath the eyelids
             We'll swear off the now
      Just waiting
Living
      Waiting

But I'm sure glad you're here.

Let her fall in love with the boy in you
But be a good enough man
To make her want to stay.

READ ALOUD WITH YOU

I just want to read out loud with you
Under the bedroom ceiling
Half dreaming
Believing in everything we say
In the hours before daylight hits
And it's just us
Testing the complete beauty
Of the energy surrounding us
Almost making sure
That it is real
It's all real
Every stagnant moment
Every sweet singular
Pause.

THE SOULD CLAP

I remember the soul clap
Like lighting under the herringbone moon
And the anchors
Dangled off your tired
With impressions of skeleton veins
On the back of fallen leaves
Where you last paused to catch up on your sleep
That face of yours
Hasn't changed in a solid thirty
And you still walk
Like you're romancing the world
With that bobby lee swagger
As the darts all fall
And melt like chests
As tongues press
Pure as the sands of deserted islands
Free hearts
On the big screen of your life
Elevating
Everything you touch.

SANDCASTLE

I don't know what it is about me
That let me break when you left.
I wanted too much.
I tend to get like that
When I feel things slipping.
Get a grip,
Regain your footing
-make sure we don't fall
We aren't supposed to fall
Unless we can do it together
And lie there
To look up
And dream again.

I think sometimes all we can do
Is to try to see the beauty
In the collapse-
As much as we did in the building.
Try to picture our creation
Washing away gradually
Like a sandcastle
By sparkling waves.
So, when you leave me, and I inevitably break
Do it slow
Like the ocean.
Remember I am fragile and delicate
As compounded sand in the sun
And remember the joy we had
Building our castle
Because even when it has fallen
And is all washed away-
The imprint in time
The hands that sculpted
Will still
Always be ours.

THE WIND JUST SAID YOUR NAME

Across fields of wonder
Feet hanging
Out of the car window
Music matching
The passing landscapes
And the world at your toes
       -sipping cascading sensations
Adventure calls

And I think
The wind
       Just said your name.

THE AWAKE IN ME

You are the awake in me
Through my days
The force
Behind my dreams
The push
In the vibrations
Within my voice
When I speak
You are the passions
In my mind
And chest
The believer
In real
In truth
And beauty

You are
The life in me.

Love
Is what you have
When two people
Mix equal parts
Madness
Trust
Loyalty
& lust.

CARRY ME WITH YOU

Carry me with you
Let's forge new paths
And scream our identities
At the world
Through the unrolled windows
Of our cars

Pushing against heavy wind
Of the long world
Unmasking new territory
For us to have
        Between one another
As a memory
Like a photograph
I'll keep
In the shoebox
Of my ever-impressionable mind.

COUNTRYSIDE PORCHES

The lights of the countryside porches
Continue to sparkle in the soft night sky
        to my excitement.

The wind in my face-
No longer such a young man anymore.

But to find such a connection
With the heavenly beauties of life
On a summer evening
        -rallying towards the zeniths
And coasting on them
As long as the ride allows
-beside myself with joy,
Trying to explain
What the rush is all about
To a worthy companion

The air is different out there
As you step off the plane in the west
        -it stares right into your soul
        If you let it.

Let it carry you
And remember the feeling
As it stands
Sigh at the amazing life ahead of us
Behind us
Within us
Surrounding us
                And touch it
Feel,
Feel.

613 BLOOMFIELD

We would leave
No star unturned
From our view on the roof

Summer bodies
Ever so slightly
Sticking to the roof tar
Heated by day
Cooling it by night
That sense
Of wonder and calm
So tied into one-
Occasionally pointing up
Out of reflex
For a flying star

These nights weren't dreams
Although
One day they will vaguely seem so

Red wine lit our faces
The time passed so slow
She said she knew
The stars danced
When
We leave them alone.

DRIFTER

If you would have told me
When I first went out into the world
On my own
For good-
With my only direction
Being the compass
In my heart,
While drifting
Like a loose leaf in the wind

That I would find myself,
Or still be here in one piece-

I never would have believed you.

Shoot for the stars darling.
If you miss- well,
At least you had your head up.

HAND ON THE WHEEL

Suicide doors
And the avenue is ripe.
My plight takes flight
In ambition and raw steam.
Hugging corners
With an unconcerned peripheral-
High-up in the archway
Loosely ground light fixtures
Flickering, acting as mistletoe
Tonight.

Elsewhere in my mind
As I hunch over the steering wheel-
The bottom of my forearm rests on top.
My fingers loose
And relaxed
All I know is road
And music-
5 dollar bill origami in the ashtray
expired insurance in the glove
                    all the windows down
pushing gas
ol' leadfoot
-with the tickets to corroborate

I don't care what I see.
I don't care where I go.
I just need to move.

BEAUTIFUL AND FADING

The way that I see it
And oh, I know
That there are millions of ways
To see it
I see it
As a piece of art
That is never finished
That the artist struggles with every day
To perfect
Adding new touches
Whenever the desire is strong
Or when free will dissolves
And animal instinct takes over
Sometimes
Even trying
To take some things away
To make for new
Or to achieve something different
For the piece may never be finished
Long after the artist dies
The creation may live on
I see life this way
Perfectly unfinished
Beautiful and fading
All at once.

FOR PETER

Another birthday of yours
Has passed.
I remember last year
I left a message for you
Talking about
How beautiful your poetry is-
And we all know
That beauty just isn't the word-
Irreplaceable is more appropriate.

The same fire born into me,
And almost in the same era.
Before your acting
And during your act-
The hourglass had minding eyes,
Such unforgettable minding eyes,
Hurdling ourselves
Among the rubble
Of time's collective mind-
Ideas
And every, last thing
among us too

As only this finite
Ever-fading time
Would allow.

STRING OF LIGHTS

If you remember anything about me-
I hope it is for the way
I pulled the stars out of you-
Then strung them in the sky
And gently
Tilted back your head
To make sure
You would never be able to forget
How beautiful you are
Inside and out.

HER OWN REFLECTION

I wonder what she sees
When she looks intently
At my eyes.
I wonder if she sees
All of the heartache
All of the love
All of the broken hearts
All of the dreams
And all of the things
That I have learned to overcome.
Or
Is all that's left
Her own reflection
Because of what these things
Have ripped out of me
Over time.

Darling-
Aim to be as easy on the soul,
As you are on the eyes

TRANSLATIONS

There will be words
Spoken between us
That are only for us
Sacred speech
Translated and remembered
By each of us differently

I can only hope you understand me
And remember me
As I intended–
Because we all hear things differently
And look back
And feel what we heard and saw
With different eyes and ears.

I just need
To push my heart upon yours
So you can feel my truths bumping
Against yours
And allow our eyes and hands
To work past the barriers
Of language and translation
So our love
Could never be confused.

LIVING

Living
Is what happens when
You experience being present
And are conscious of it
While still going
Through the motions
Of everyday life.

Until then,
You only exist.

MONSTERS

I've spent so much
Of my life
Mastering the pain

I'm numb now

It's okay to come close

I've learned
To bite
Only when provoked
Or bitten first

This is what life
Comes to

Circling
Over the beaten monsters
Inside of us

Which like in a dream
We can
Never seem to kill.

EMPTINESS

Love has a way
Of disguising flaws-
Staying places
A little longer
Than we probably should,
Finding positives
Where only hurt lies,
And being hard on ourselves
For being the unique holder
Of an affection
So deep and unexpected
That we can get lost fully
In the emptiness
Of another's
Arms.

I've been so damn busy
Living
In the here and now–
It has always been
Almost impossible
For me to make plans
For tomorrow

And I must say,
I like it
That way.

DE J A VU

I'm remembering you
As if
I had been with you all along.
When you have that flash
Of a beautiful time
   And you chase it
   Over and over
   In your mind.
Lining things up,
Starting from the beginning
Again, again-
Trying to prolong the thought.
Trying to hold on.
To feel it,
All over again.

It was you.

OUR OLD SOULS

We will fall into one another
Where the lines of time
Cross themselves
And the day
Lands at our feet.
It is just time between us
Ahead of us
Behind us
Everywhere.
And we went
Leaning into our feelings
Of all that we ever wanted-
Making way for the change
That is in the air
Coming to calmly cling to our skin.
Our old souls
And our tired faces
Allowing us to breathe again
In the symphony of creation
And its sudden movements.
I am just waiting   and being
Against the odds

Still pushing
Kicking
Pulling
Dreaming
Crashing
Burning
Living
Dying
Laughing
Crying.

CRUSHING ROSES

A guy walks into a bar
A very deliberate walk
Peaceful
Yet full of intention.

As he walks past the table
That I'm sitting at,
I notice the duffel bag that
He is carrying.
It's open
At the zipper on top.
What's inside is the important part-
                                    Roses's.

Stems cut off almost wholly,
Rose's.
A duffel bag full.

I get up to go to the bathroom
I do the 100' walk
Up the stairs
Back through the crowded bar
To my table-
I make my way through obnoxious drunks
And sweethearts alike.
As I walk
I feel like I'm stepping on things.
                                    Rose's.

Rose's all over the floor,
Everywhere.
It was a miracle of sorts-
And I thought to myself
How beautiful this interesting gesture is-

To throw roses all over the floor

Of this random Irish pub on Ludlow.

That night I felt love.
Not the love from another person's touch
Or their words-
Love in a simpler form
Symbolic and sweet
A love among humanity

Strong in the world.

RUN

Don't look back.
Eyes forward,
Heart like an arrow,

Let it spin
Out of control
Behind you

Sometimes
You just
Have to
Run.

YOUR SONG

You are everything that
I never expected
Hugging the edge
Of my infinities
Twirling about
In succession
With the electric planet
In slow motion
Dedicating
Your song to me.

Stay close to me
And I promise
I will never
Let you
Stop dreaming.

171,476

171,476 words
In the English language.

Yet none of them
Can accurately describe
The way the energy
Inside of me
Starts to glow and radiate
When you are near.

Lord,
If I do anything else
Before I die-
Let me find a way
To properly explain to you
How much
I love her.

FATED

Hotel rooms
Late night plans
To douse
And swish
Only the finest
Post-prohibition
Grains
Staring out
That hotel window
When my song comes on
And we're deep course
In our lovemaking
And it hits me
With the finest vibrations
I'm high
As high as I have ever been
My brain
Is like a pinball machine
Euphoria
Utter and complete
I look down
And say
I never want
This moment to end
But the song is almost over
The sun starts
To perk
The alcohol
Is wearing off
Her arched back relaxes
And we kiss hard-
Time for descent.

We are such pretty, daring, little creatures.

SICK

I'm sick of
Fast food
Fast people
Fast music
Get rich quick schemes
Technology
That fast life
Man
I'm feeling like
Slowing down
Listening harder
Being distracted less
Less phones
And screens
Less drink
And drugs
Less running away

More running towards
Myself

More substance
Less abuse.

You just have to believe me.
The world is waiting
Ever so anxiously
For your touch.

TAKE ON THE WORLD

Is it
      The restless wanderer in me
Is it
      The energy of the universe
Talking to me in
Its unique, perfect tongue

There is a call in me to go
To rush out into
All of it-
To take on the world

Better yet,
      To be
      in all of the world
      While I'm here

I want all of the tastes,
Smells and adventures
To become a part of me
      All of who I am

So I went.
I went,
And this is what happened.

SWEET DARLINGS OF THE RENAISSANCE

Sweet darlings of the renaissance
Watchers of the Heron's weave and bob
The starling diaries and grass-swept feet
Of the fountains first kiss
At the Emory ball
Pretty little high notes
Tugging at the baby's breath
Take me- to live the promise
Of realities grandeur
Between the open pages
Of large books
Encased in glass-
        Look but don't touch.
For our minds wander
In the crystal ware of the lighthouse
Waiting to be broken
To steer in the steamships by hand-
As the dove's fly free
And as it happens
Dripping wet lips
-purse from high above
To push through the valance of clouds
And aim for the sphere
All while I wait in line at a deli
-for my sandwich –
It's all happening,
My sweet darlings of the renaissance.

We are all trapped
Between the dancing shadows
& starbursts
Behind our eyelids-
And the absolute madness
That is the life
On the other side of them.

OUR GODLY HEARTS

All I want
Is to watch the child wonder at the sky
Because that child is who I want to be
And I watch brave women holding hands
Walk past
      and I love them for it
All of the faces
The poetry
The life
The death
It will get me
      But they'll never take me alive

I'm going down
Pen-clenched
Cigarette burning
With the danger of magnetic fields
Crossing our hearts
Hoping to never die-completely
Only to fulfill our dreams
In the painstaking drama
Of a play
That is our lives

And the sudden rush of humanity
That caresses our insides forever
Dancing around our godly hearts
May make the world
Catch its ground
Feel the fire
      Run with it
      I beg you.

THE BREAK

There is a breaking right now
In me
A change in the course
Of my propelling energy
      It chases
The very last moment
The feelings
The warm of my chest
My perception
      It chases
      It all away
It is the breaking
Of the last
To present to me
The new
And I endure it
Observe it
Welcome it

I suppose
It will be the break
In me,
The breaks of me
That build
What you see.

LUSTER

Just look at what has endured
Little lessons
That turn into champagne floats
Exercises in happiness
Pain that's bled through
Minor details
Last minute plans
That turn lifetimes
Upside down
On the never-ending curved stone
Upon which we reside
Looping memories
Read back verbatim to friends
And loved ones
Scanning one another's eyes for hints
Of emotion and wonder
Taking our time to be ourselves
With one another
In the dance
Of dreaming luster.

All is not fair
In love and in war.
Never give someone
Who broke your heart
The chance to break it
Again.
That's like giving your weapon
To the enemy
While crossing
Your fingers.

SHADOW BOXING

I've been shadow boxing
With myself
For such a long time
Questioning everything that I do
Swinging away freely
Hard
And often.
Wrestling with the worst parts
And the best–
Never really knowing the right
And wrong of it all
And too punch-drunk
To keep score anymore.
I'm just tired of fighting
And it always seems
Like another round
Is about to start–
  Fuck it,
  Let's do this.

A BLOOM

I hope she's got a killer smile
Because I don't.
I hope she has the kind of beauty that
Pushes out of her
Like flowers
In a well-cared for garden.
I hope she has a hard time
Letting me go to work
In the morning
But enough confidence to know
That I'll be there
Waiting for her
When she gets home.
I hope she feels me
When I touch her
And that she knows
What I'm trying to touch
Is so much more than skin.
I hope we figure out a way
To stick by each other
Until all of the days
Fade away.

NEVER LEAVE MY SIDE

I just need to hear it one more time.
Tell me like the way you used to
And grab my hand
That little way you do.
Fix my hair real quick
Just how you like it.
Blow that eyelash off my cheek
With your sweet breath.
One hand on my chest,
Lips on my neck,
Just tell me one more time
That you will
Never leave my side.

You, old soul
Are a light
A vessel of constant refraction
So bright
-a crystal on the sill at noon

Luminous and radiant
Creating more light
Wherever you go.

You wanted my magic.
I wanted your sweet soul,
naked and free.

EVERYTHING TO DO WITH YOU

The nights are so much sweeter with you.
The days so much brighter.
My whole life feels lighter.
My laugh
A little more real, and stronger.
The air just tastes cleaner.
The water more pure.

And I'm sure
It has everything
To do with you.

SO MUCH TO GIVE

I have so much to give
And I have given all of it
So many times, throughout my life
You'd think I'd be done
That I would be spent
Nothing left to give at all
After watching things crash around me so many times
But I'm here
It's not as simple
as being tough or stubborn
It's not as easy
As me being innocent or naïve
In fact
I am all of it
I am everything
My spirit is a fire
That continues to burn in the rain
My heart is a dagger
Wrapped in roses
My eyes are the caretakers
Of all they see.

You see,
I love
With everything I have
Because I know there is no other way
I refuse to be halfway there
And I need you to be the same way
If my roses
Are going to grow in your garden
I wont stop giving everything I have
Even if its not you
Who gets to receive it anymore
I am forever unbroken

Because even as things fall apart
I was built to place them back together
At the exact same time.

I have found in me myself
And my heart
Will continue to be my compass
Even as the powerful magnets of the world
Pull me
In one thousand different directions
At once.
Inside,
Through it all
I will have my peace.
And I will manage to love
Until the end of time.

While you're at it-
Live life
as beautifully
As you possibly can.